"TENACITY"

From Welfare To Business Owner

A Mental Challenge Too!

By Donna Dorothy Barker

Now I wasn't always mentally challenged

but as a kid I always thought I was a loner.

There was always something different

about me. Even though I knew this it

definitely made me more of a go getter.

I sought to challenge myself as much as

I could because I knew that someday it

would all stop...come to a halt.. How or

for what means I didn't know but who

cared..I hoped for the best.

I studied gymnastics and dancing , guitar

baton twirling , art, mathematics and

always had a positive attitude so therefore

I always had friends.

My family was great..my neighborhood

also had lots of great people so how and

why things would change for me I couldn't tell you.

My Dad and brother built a beautiful, big

house for all 7 of us to live in and life

for me was only getting better and better

every year.

But then something happened..my parents

divorced... Then.. yes..started marijuana.

I was young..it was the end of highschool.

Then college came a year after I worked

from graduating H.S. but the drugs didn't.

I went to start my first year of college

in Hawaii and well...that was where I suffered

my first mental breakdown.... I was 6000 miles

away from home and started psychotherapy.. What?!

I was running out of money and out of my

mind...I flew home and took a little R&R ..

I took a walk in my neighborhood and

tried to get my life together by

thinking of a plan. My Dad was gone,

no money coming in and my sister was

still in grade school..

I got a restaurant job and started Russian

studies at a local college...It was great.

My life was great again!!...I was going

places , doing important things..! I

even got a job at the UN in Manhattan!

I could remember Christmas celebrations

that were finally fun ! Just like when I was a kid

but without Dad this time it wasn't really

as unfortunate as I expected! I even quit drugs!!

I continued my studies but then tough

times came to our life as a family again..

Being that not enough money was coming

in my Mom had no choice but to sell the

house.

She sold it and took a rental close by

so my sister could finish school.

Man..moving out of that house was a real

downer. I really got severely depressed

so during school at college I sought

more council to get me though it.

I felt my mind was scrambling for

answers and I was on overdrive to

get my studies done and working

crazy hours at night...what was once

a dream come true was slowly turning

into that nightmare I was
running from that

I knew as kid.!..I was running
and running!

It was catching up around every
corner!

No money, just work, and work..
study and study...a vicious cycle
in my

head of scrambling eggs frying
away

probably from those years of using

drugs I would surmise.

Mom ran out of money..we moved to

a tiny house and I had to

 start taking meds and go on welfare...

State insurance for my doctors and

just walking away from the happiness I once had. I never cried though..I knew

I did everything for myself to stay proud up to that point so I learned a word that kept me going on my quest to a normal life:

"TENACITY!!!" So many people were

making me feel like I was nothing but

lazy and that I should work because

being Bipolar is no excuse. No it's not

an excuse but what it is is a lousy way

to feel about yourself..a freaking mental

case! I lost all confidence inside and

even though I took good care of myself

in my appearance and physical well

being I was an emotional wreck.!

Insecure and at the bottom.

Then this happens..a girlfriend I knew

in High school said to me when I told her

of my bipolar disorder that all of her life

she had an Aunt that was Bipolar too but

was always ashamed of it!...That's why

she never told me about her!..okay..not

a friend there..NEXT!!..but this stigma

sucks...! It's a bad state and it feels

like that even worse when you go to the

doctors office and have to show them a

State medical insurance card...HUMILIATING!!

I'd get this: " Oh, we don't accept that insurance Mame, you have to go to a clinic!"
(Keep Tenacious Donna).

Also another incident during a hospital stay...I was getting a medication change and had to stay hospitalized for

for a few days. Well, the social worker lady called me in her office for a meeting to get to know me and place me into a job after I went home. So, she asked me about my education and

work history.. This is what I told her:

1: Started college in Honolulu

2: Attended College at SUNY

Stonybrook holding a Russian major

3: Attended The Russian School in Vermont

4: Worked at the UN

5: Took time off to work at the Minskoff theater in a Dance Company that we did National TV appearances

6: Resumed Russian study

and that's when I had my
mental breakdown.

Well, she said that she
didn't believe one word I
said and that she wanted my
Mother's phone number. I gave
it to her and left.

Well, according to my mother
the social worker was laughing
on the phone saying

that my mother wouldn't
believe how delusional I was!
She told my Mom everything
I claimed I did and was laughing!
My Mother said
that everything Donna said
was true and I did not make
anything up.
The Social Worker was
humiliated and completely
shot down. My Mom then

told the woman not to put
Mentally challenged people
all in one lump.
I'm tell you this (my readers)
because sometimes staying
"Tenacious" you must walk
with a great deal of faith. Faith
in God and Family and
Friends. Nonetheless , my life
went on..not walking away but
from that? I ran!

So, taking meds for years and doing things to keep busy like yard work , reading books , studying Russian etc..then suddenly

out of the blue my Mom gets diagnosed

with Colon Cancer..!..Took years of

chemotherapy and radiation therapy

but she got through it.... Then she got

Shingles and suffered real bad from the pain from

that and well the last 5 years of her life

was spent fighting breast cancer.

It was during those years that my life

turned around for me..I began writing

books mostly my memoirs and poetry.

I wrote up to about 20 books and

they didn't sell much but my Mom

was thrilled and seeing her happy was

priceless. As a matter of fact I also

started to feel better inside from this

so I'd write some funny jokes here and

there and take them to Coffee Shop

Open mic nights and tell them in front of an

audience on video camera for the

sole reason of showing Mom when

I got home!...She gave me reason

to hold "Tenaciously" to my goals and

when I'd get down about something she'd

often say: "Don't give up that ship!"

Rest on Peace Mom..Now I cry a lot folks...

She died of a stroke at 82 years old and

It's 3 years now since she's gone to

heaven..so now that her job is done...

my job gets started..!!!..I dropped my State

medical insurance and went on an

affordable plan..My Social worker at the

state office was so happy for me she

actually cried!..I'm still disabled though

and I know that I always will be
on meds

but that Social Worker right
there proved

to me that my "Tenacity" was
working!

My Mom left the house to me
and my

sister in her Will and

Wow..so now for 3 years I kept
writing

and telling jokes, seeing my usual doctors

taking it day by day .

I even held a writing lecture at my

local library to teach writing techniques

and how to get free online publication!.

 The books that didn't sell at

the lecture I donated to

a women's shelter in NYC!.

I bought a used laptop for $80 and found

out that it has Skype on it.

I thought and thought about the education

in College I got studying the Russian

Language years ago and maybe I could use

Skype to give online lessons in beginner

courses to students!.. I mean, I can't

get a job because I can't drive a car due

to eye surgery I had years ago and I really

don't feel strong enough to work outside

the house ..I take 16 pills a day!!

I mean sometimes

I get tired !..so this idea with

Russian language

lessons seems to really be the

one for me!

I got my DBA license which was

interesting

and simple enough..I mean

figuring out the

name of the company was tougher!

Filled out other forms and then got my

business bank account and business

cards and well.....now...

I have a HOME BASED BUSINESS!!!

It's called:

"LITERALLY RUSSIAN"

I no longer feel like I have nothing to offer.

I have a real sense of confidence within

and even though it's going to take months

to get the business off the ground I'm

not paying out of pocket for it to keep it .! Social Security likes that indeed!

I charge by every 20 minutes but that's

just to get started..Things could change

and I'm ready for it!

I may be mentally challenged and caught on a little slow but...

TENACITY worked!!!!

Thanks friends and Good luck

and..Go Get 'em..!!!